CW00843202

THE RHYTHM OF WAR

IN A CIVILISED WORLD

Terence Parker

ROMANS

Published in 2007 by:

ROMANS
24 King's Road
Salisbury
Wiltshire SP1 3AD

A CIP catalogue record is available at the British Library.

ISBN 978-0-9554843-0-8

Printed in England by:

SALISBURY PRINTING
Greencroft Street
Salisbury
Wiltshire SP1 1JF

Source material has been acknowledged: in particular, the origin of each quotation. Many quotations are drawn from the nineteenth century; the remainder are limited to a few words or sentences but licences were sought for those of sufficient substance. Notwithstanding this, any person who believes that a significant infringement of rights has occurred is invited to contact the publisher.

To My Parents

This book is dedicated to the memory of **Charles Owen Parker**, the eldest son of a Northumberland railwayman, who joined the Army at the age of 14 and served in the infantry for twenty-nine years; and of his wife, **Winifred May Parker**, the daughter of a London policeman, who loyally supported her husband for thirty-eight years.

Contents

The photographs in this book were taken by the author, who also designed and produced each figure. ***A profile of the author*** *appears after the epilogue.*

Preface

The seeds of wisdom are sown less by critical studies and learned monographs than by insight, broad impressions, and flashes of intuition.

Carl Von Clauzwitz   On War

This short book reveals and explains the natural mechanism which has driven nations to war since the dawn of civilisation.

Knowledge is drawn from many seminal works. To spare the reader, the essence of each seminal work has been encapsulated within a few short paragraphs, or within a few particularly relevant quotations. This seemingly drastic condensation is necessary to draw aside the many veils of complexity which obscure an essentially simple process. Some readers may wish to explore an area of knowledge more deeply: to assist those readers, source documents have been clearly identified.

Broad impressions and flashes of intuition punctuate this book: intangible concepts are employed, bold assumptions are made and huge summations of human behaviour are presented. Reader scepticism is almost inevitable, but observation of the world and the passage of time should gradually erode that scepticism.

12th March, 2007   Terence Parker

1. INTRODUCTION

Photograph 1 One of 118 Demarcation Stones which mark the limit of the German advance in July 1918

Wars differ. Few poems emerged from the Second World War or the Korean War, but poignant verses from the First World War still evoke the sad memories which validate every Remembrance Sunday. Poetry stems from the child within us; so it would seem, from the argument in this book, did the First World War.

Sigmund Freud recognised that human behaviour during the First World War was irrational, but he could not explain the phenomenon. Freud had examined the minds and close relationships of very many individuals during his lifetime, but war is the violent expression of collective human emotion. The nature of that emotion varies with time and each one of us contributes to the collective emotion of our nation.

Using knowledge bequeathed to us by Freud and several of his contemporaries, this book explains how civilised man's innate aggression is manipulated by Nature to produce a clear pattern of individual violence, revolution and war. Figure 1 displays that pattern, which might reasonably be termed *the violence cycle.* Just how the violence cycle arises is explained in later sections of this book.

Figure 1 THE VIOLENCE CYCLE

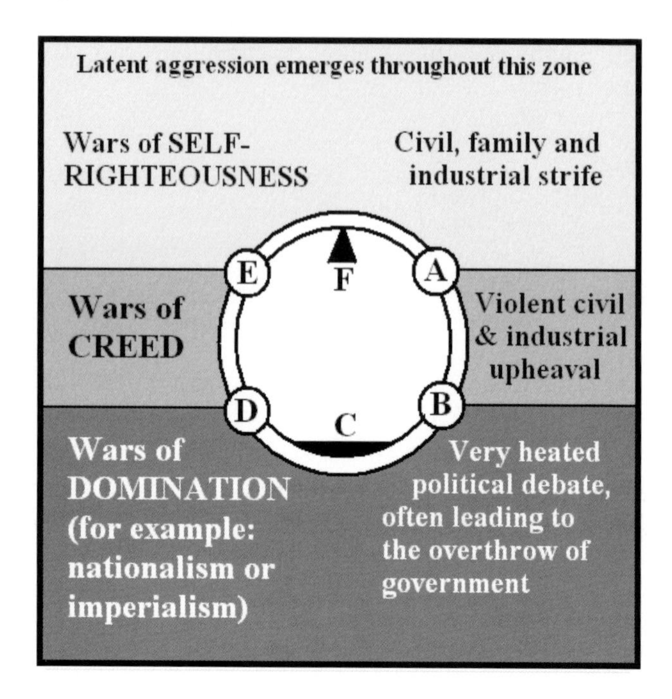

Leaders emerge, survive or are overthrown dependent upon their ability to meet the strongly felt, but often hidden desires of their nation. A nation experiencing tumultuous adversity will crave a powerful, decisive leader whereas a stable, prosperous nation might prefer an urbane, sociable leader. During a significant period of crisis (A, B, D or E on Figure 1) a nation's underlying desire may suddenly change, causing the overthrow of a monarch or head of government.

During the twentieth century, Britain suffered two catastrophic world wars, a severe depression and the often violent collapse of empire. Not surprisingly, the nation exhibited great swings of emotion. Underlying influences which might have remained hidden in a quieter period emerged in sharp contrast, presenting us with a unique opportunity to examine the behaviour of a nation.

In this book, attention is focused on Britain but man is ubiquitous. During recent years, the United States of America has become an increasingly intrusive player on the world stage. Confident and powerful, but strangely forgetful of its own conquistador past, America has sought repeatedly to impose its political creed upon other, far older cultures. While doing so, America has established its own pattern of warfare: a pattern which closely relates to that of other developed nations.

Before the reader proceeds further into this book, he or she is invited to look closely at Figure 1 with a view to identifying our present position on the violence cycle. Please be aware that there is a decade or so between each of the alphabetical points.

2. THE FUNDAMENTAL CAUSE OF WAR

Photograph 2 Cemetery Hill, Gettysburg, Pennsylvania

When we review European and North American wars later in this book, two facts will become evident: firstly, that most wars occur during a long period of rising prosperity; secondly, that the most lethal wars occur near the top of that rise.

Figure 2 illustrates the second phenomenon: each of the wars shown occurred in the latter part of a prolonged period of rising prosperity. The wars and dates will be examined in more detail later but we can see, for example, that the 1914-18 First World War occurred toward the end of the period 1896 to 1920.

Figure 2 WARS OCCURRING TOWARD THE ENDS OF FOUR PERIODS OF RISING PROSPERITY

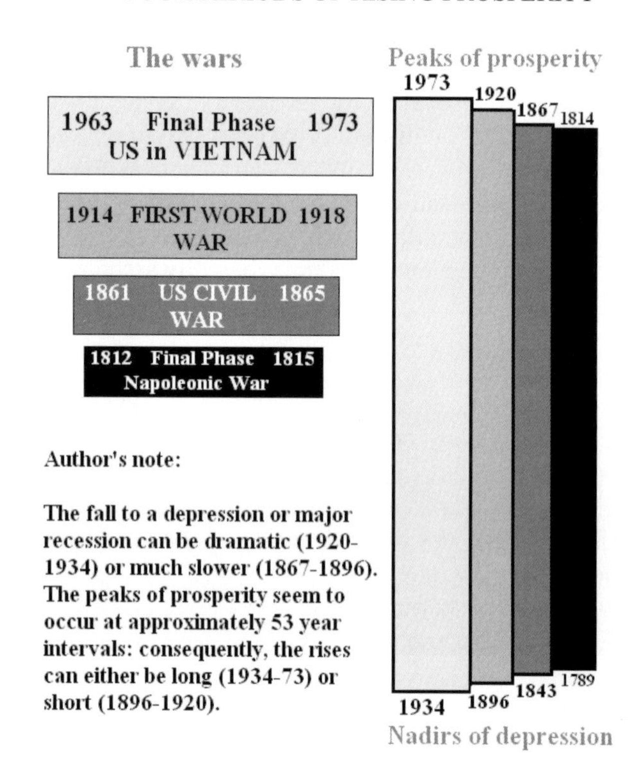

But how do we define and measure prosperity? The English dictionary [(1)] tells us that people are prosperous when they *have money and everything that is needed for a good life.*

Economists monitor the level of prosperity using the commodity index: a price index based upon the cost of raw materials fuelling industry (for example, iron ore) or satisfying consumer demand (for example, coffee).

As the level of prosperity rises, the demand for raw materials increases, elevating the prices of those raw materials; these price elevations combine to raise the commodity index. The end of that prosperity rise is marked by a levelling off of the commodity index, prior to its subsequent decline.

We might reasonably assume that prolonged prosperity stems from civilisation. Without civilisation there would be no prosperity, because people would be insufficiently well-organised to undertake the necessary trade and manufacturing, or insufficiently socially developed to enjoy the culture generally associated with prosperity.

If civilisation encourages rising prosperity, it must also promote war, because, as Figure 2 reveals, the most devastating wars occur at the end of a period of rising prosperity. In reality, almost all major wars between developed nations occur within successive periods of rising prosperity, the nature of each war being determined by its position on a particular rise. We must conclude, therefore, that civilisation itself is the fundamental cause of war in a civilised world.

Some might argue that wars take place between poor tribal groups in Africa and Afghanistan. As we shall see later, the nature of war changes as prosperity increases: if an uncivilised group's prosperity fails to increase, the group's urge to dominate will continue to promote war.

Others might note that some civilised nations, such as Switzerland, avoid war. This seems to have been achieved by Switzerland's enduring moderate prosperity and its successful avoidance of military alliance. Both factors disrupt the cause of war.

Notwithstanding these anomalies, the basic premise that civilisation is the fundamental cause of war appears correct. This premise is important, if only to negate Karl Marx's view that capitalism, alone, is the cause of war. Wrong assumptions lead to wrong conclusions and ineffective war prevention measures. The recent decline of communism seems to confirm this.

What are the right conclusions? Why is it that so many prosperous nations do resort to war? What are the destructive forces within a civilised nation? How do these forces encourage war? These questions are answered in the sections which follow.

Reference:

(1) *Longman Dictionary of Contemporary English* Third Edition (definition of prosperity)

3. CIVILISATION

Photograph 3 Historic marker, Huntsville, Alabama

One might characterise civilisation as a large, sophisticated, well-regulated group of human beings engaged in the fruitful pursuit of knowledge, enjoyment of the arts, production of goods and trade with other such groups.

Civilised groups develop hierarchies and privileged institutions: typically government office holders, learned professionals, and their associated bureaucracies. Many of these people and institutions aid the creation of wealth, usually through capitalism. Other people and institutions, including some of the most prestigious, will be consumers rather than creators of wealth.

Karl Marx [(1)] presented the rather narrow view that "*capitalist production begets, with the inexorability of a law of Nature, its own negation*". Were he alive today, he would probably realise that communism, too, begets its own negation. In truth, any natural system, including civilisation, will beget its own negation. What we see is a rather nebulous example of the fundamental truth: to every action there is an equal and opposite reaction

The very nature of man brings about his own regulation, because, as Charles Darwin [(3)] explained: "*In the case of every species, many different checks, acting at different periods of life, and during different seasons or years, probably come into play; some one check or some few being generally the most potent, but all concurring in determining the average number or even the existence of the species*". We humans may consider ourselves more sophisticated than the ants, and more important than the two hundred year old, two hundred foot high trees which tower above us, but we are still governed by Nature's laws.

Despite Marx's concern, capitalism alone cannot be regarded as the self-regulating mechanism of civilisation because it is insufficiently inclusive. Socio-economics (the study of human behaviour and its relationship with economics) offers the best insight into civilisation's self regulation. Friedrich Engels[(2)] linked socio-economics to civilisation when he offered "*the palpable but previously overlooked fact that men must first eat, drink, have shelter and clothing, therefore must* *work, before they can fight for domination, pursue politics, religion, philosophy, etc".*

Labour, management, hierarchies, prestigious institutions, leadership, and political struggle - Right versus Left – are the fundamental elements of socio-economics, but it is the relative balance of production over consumption which determines a nation's overall prosperity at any particular moment. Civilisation gives rise to many costly, unproductive consumers. Adam Smith[4] helpfully described them for us: "*some of the gravest and most important, and some of the most frivolous professions; churchmen, lawyers, physicians, men of letters of all kinds: players, buffoons, musicians, opera singers, ballet dancers, etc*".

As societies emerge from a depression and get richer, culture blossoms, hierarchies grow, and the sophisticated prosper. During the early stages, industrial and agricultural production, too, will grow, allowing the demands of the unproductive to be met.

When memory of the depression fades, confidence continues to grow but commitment wanes. Both productive and unproductive people become more demanding. As their often noisy demands are met, productivity falters. Despite this, people still clamour for higher wages and grants, better working conditions and a larger slice of the national cake. The 'all pull together' attitude of the depression years evaporates, leaving selfishness in its place. Consequently, productivity and prosperity start to decline. This decline continues until the next depression is reached, when the socio-economic 'long cycle' starts all over again.

It is this long cycle which readily accepts the seeds of war, nurtures them over a decade or so, and then allows them to germinate in the warmth of prosperity.

References:

(1) *Karl Marx and Friedrich Engels*
Basic writings on Politics and Philosophy
(Collins 1959), Page 11.

(2) As above, Page 18.

(3) *The Origin of Species (ChapterIII)*
Charles Darwin (John Murray 1859)

(4) *The Wealth of Nations* Adam Smith 1776
Book 2, Chapter III.

4. THE LONG CYCLE

Photograph 4 Part of a Manchester mural

The last section explained very briefly why the long cycle occurs. In essence: economic adversity instills diligence and integrity, thus encouraging effective production; the resultant prosperity erodes diligence and integrity but inflates grandeur, causing productivity and then prosperity to decline; prosperity's decline leads us back, eventually, to adversity. History suggests that the period of the long cycle is a little over fifty years.

On Figure 3a, the black circle ABCDEFA represents one complete revolution of the long cycle. Were we to put a one-year date against each alphabetical milestone of the last complete revolution, we might see:

C	1934	(and then1995)
D	1947	(and then 2001)
E	1963	
F	1973	
A	1980	
B	1987	

Date selection is necessarily imprecise but, as we shall see later, there are a few clear indicators.

Figure 3a THE LONG CYCLE

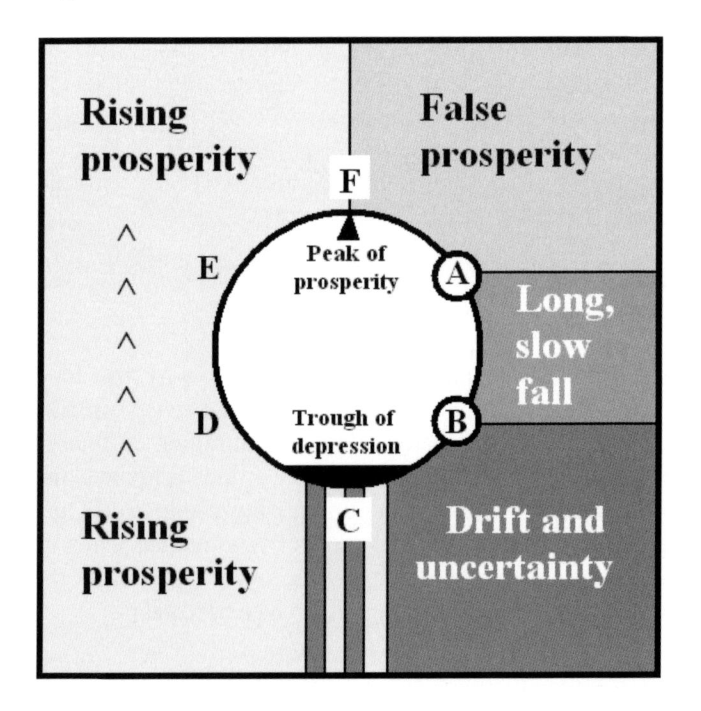

To facilitate cross-referencing, the milestone lettering remains the same throughout this book. In later sections, milestones A, B, D and E are each 'stretched' to span two years to more accurately define periods of transition.

If we leave aside the cause of the long cycle and look only at the outcome, we see the sequence displayed in Figure 3a. This circular portrayal will allow us to relate the cycle to human behaviour in a later section. The information on Figure 3a is drawn, in the main, from papers by Kondratieff [(1)] and Kaiser [(2)]. Kondratieff's paper has provided the bedrock for many later socio-economic papers; Kaiser's paper examines the decline of prosperity more closely. Both papers deal mainly with finance - prices, inflation and interest rates - but Kondratieff also commented on certain aspects of human behaviour. In particular, he noted an apparent, but unexplained relationship between war and the long cycle. The main purpose of this book is to further expose, and then explain, that relationship.

Point C is the centre of the trough of depression. This trough is one of a succession of prolonged periods of lethargy during which world trade subsides to its lowest level. The occurrence of these troughs appears irregular and imprecise: looking back we might place C in 1995, 1934, 1896, 1849 and 1789. Depressions vary in severity but, as we shall see in a later section, even the very mild 1990s 'depression' seemed to affect behaviour in Britain and America.

Let us follow the nation as it emerges from a depression and then passes through each successive phase of the economic long cycle, beginning with rising prosperity:

Figure 3b RISING PROSPERITY

You may be enjoying this zone at present. It is a generally favourable period punctuated by minor recessions: typically the five-year election-related business cycle.
(BUT: beware of a minor financial crash akin to 1906!)

For the next two decades we should expect to experience increasing, but fluctuating inflation; increasing interest rates; and falling unemployment.

Wars might interfere but the rise will continue until Point F, most probably 2026.

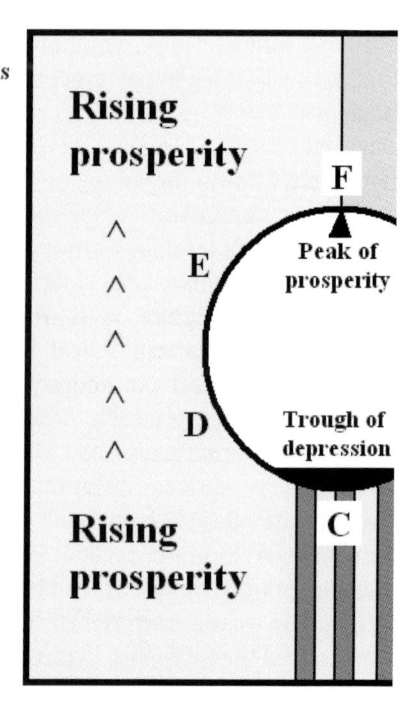

At each successive <u>peak of prosperity</u> (F), there is a very pronounced commodity index peak. This peak reflects a very high demand for commodities (wheat, oil, timber, iron ore, etc) to satisfy the final surge of world-wide commerce before it falters, tries unsuccessfully to recover, and then declines. Debt escalation, rampant inflation and high interest rates will, by then, have severely wounded the world economy. The economy will continue to decline, apart from one brief surge, until attitudes change several decades later.

These peaks of prosperity at F appear to be one of life's

few certainties; they occur regularly at about 53 year intervals: ...1814, 1867, 1920, 1973 ....2026? Why is this? We don't know, but the interval might relate to man's lifespan and may be governed by the sunspot cycle. Furthermore, unscrupulous financiers might be 'sharpening' the price spike by pulling it into synchronism with the anticipated year. They could do this by enthusiastically encouraging people to buy commodities until a particular year, and then suddenly offloading their own substantial holding: this would trigger the anticipated collapse. Viewed around the world, the various regional and specific (for example, petroleum product) commodity index peaks may be offset by a few years, but the 53 year intervals are surprisingly consistent.

After the steep, exciting final rise, the nation reaches the peak of prosperity but, before it can enjoy the moment, it falls into the maelstrom of false prosperity:

Figure 3c FALSE PROSPERITY

A very unsettled period: wild speculation; high peaks of inflation; very high interest rates; commodity price instability; faltering production and the onset of high unemployment.

Production recovers half-heartedly just before Point A.

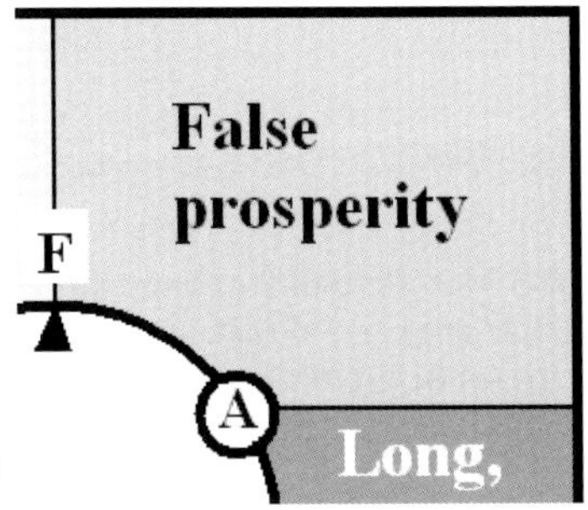

Point A may be likened to the brick wall of a bank, against which excited governments and industrialists beat their fists, as they attempt to get their hands on the money within. But, badly mauled by debt defaulters and currency speculators, the world's banks have either collapsed or grown wiser: consequently, loans are resolutely withheld or very strictly prescribed.

Disillusioned and increasingly resentful, the nation passes beyond Point A, and enters the long, slow fall to depression:

Figure 3d THE LONG, SLOW FALL

A seemingly chaotic period characterised by relentlessly increasing unemployment and decreasing inflation.

The nation's economy may be likened to a punctured balloon which defies even the most heated attempts to re-inflate it.

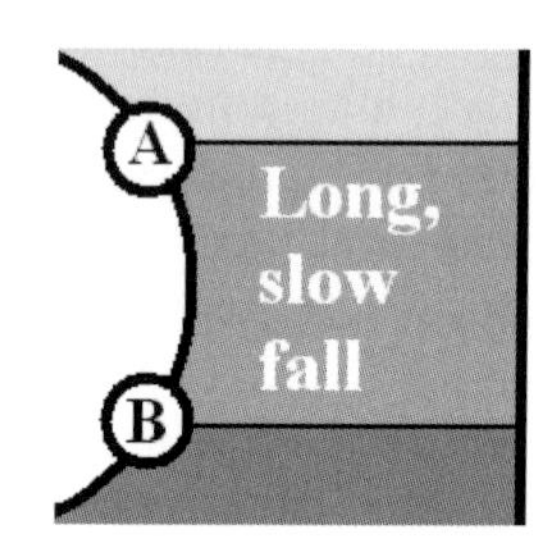

The stock market crashes near Point B. This acts as a rather ineffective brake on the decline, which continues more slowly:

Figure 3e DRIFT AND UNCERTAINTY

Political argument continues to inhibit recovery; slowly but surely attitudes begin to change and common sense emerges.

In the meantime, land and house prices fall; followed, eventually, by interest rates.

At Point C, production and prosperity begin to rise again.

fall
B
C
Drift and uncertainty

Points A, B, D and E are the four most influential points on the cycle as far as war is concerned. The nation's passage down through points A and B is normally marked by a crescendo of noisy riots, but the nation rises almost silently through points D and E. More will be said about these four points later.

Each generation of the nation is born at some point on the long cycle; each goes on to experience the cycle's varying benevolence and adversity. During its formative decades, each generation acquires an indelible imprint which influences its behaviour in later decades. These varying imprints, within successive generations, produce our ever-changing nation and, working together, they give rise to a cycle of human behaviour. We will examine this *human cycle* in the next section.

Within the *human cycle*, which is closely allied to the economic *long cycle*, we will find violent elements. By isolating these violent elements, we can produce the *violence cycle:* the template which allows us to examine the nature, timing and primary cause of specific exemplary wars.

References:

(1) *The Long Waves in Economic Life*
(*Dei Langen Wellen der Konjunctur*)
N D Kondratieff, Archiv fur Sozialwissenschaft und Sozialpolitick, 56:573-609, 1926.

A translation appeared within *The HARVARD Review of Economic Statistics Volume XVII, Nov 1935, Number 6.*
The paper is available on the internet:
http://www.kwaves.com/kwave.pdf

(2) *The Kondratieff Cycle* R W Kaiser ,
Financial Analysts' Journal May-June 1979

5. THE HUMAN CYCLE

Photograph 5 Instructional plaque: medieval stone masons at work

When ice is warmed, it melts into water; when water is heated, it evaporates into steam. If we look at human behaviour, we see a similar process. During periods of economic depression the nation is united: people are held together by a common desire to survive adversity. As prosperity 'warms' the nation, it melts into groups. When even greater prosperity 'heats' the groups, they evaporate into free, unfettered individuals. These individuals remain free and unfettered until prosperity declines, when the reverse occurs.

Figure 4a displays the human (behaviour) cycle. The three horizontal layers represent the three population states. The circles A, B D and E represent four 'periods of crisis' during which break-up or coalescing occurs: the dates shown follow the 1930s depression; the most recent revolution would show Point D as 2001-2002.

Figure 4a THE HUMAN CYCLE

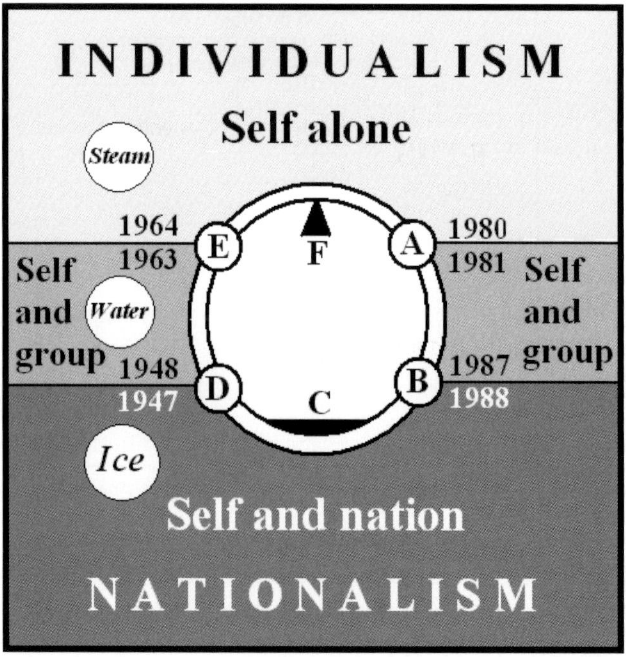

INDIVIDUALISM
Self alone
Steam
1964 E F A 1980
Self 1963 1981 Self
and Water and
group 1948 1987 group
D C B
1947 1988
Ice
Self and nation
NATIONALISM

Periods of crisis

During each of the four periods of crisis, civilised man seems to experience an emotional surge, akin to adolescence or the menopause. Furthermore, after each crisis period there is a noticeable change in his attitude and behaviour. The emotional surge reveals itself as near-concurrent peaks in several seemingly unrelated statistics, for example: births, suicides and the numbers of workers on strike.

Figure 5 EMOTION-RELATED STATISTICS FOR THE PERIOD 1925-1985

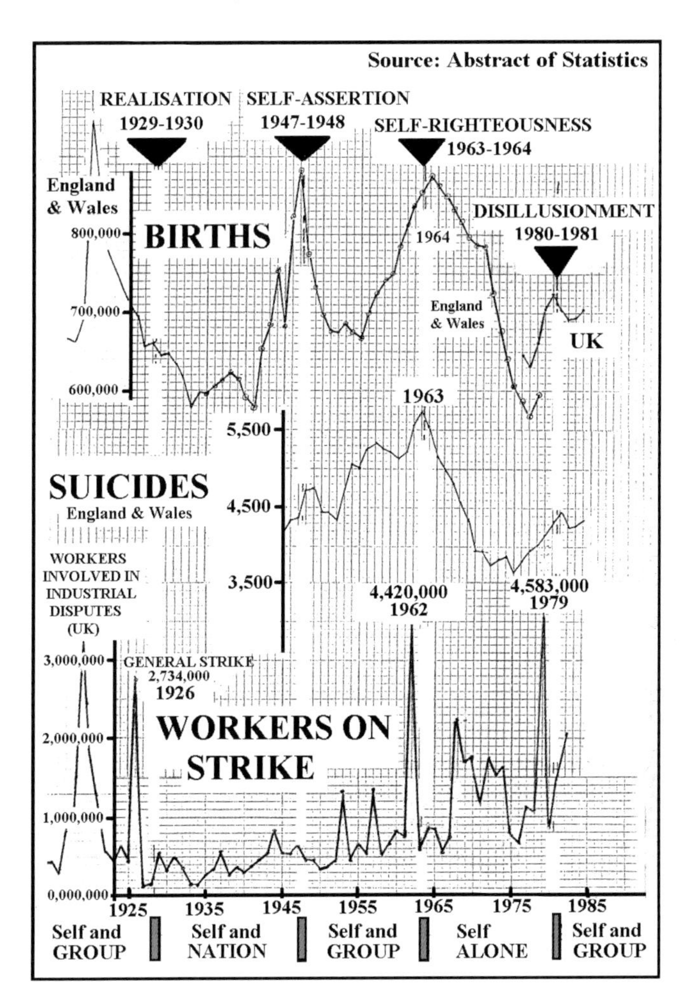

Figure 5 shows the variation of these emotion-related statistics during the period 1925 to 1985. UK includes England, Wales, Scotland and Northern Ireland. We can see, for example, that all three statistics peak within a year of 1963: workers 62; suicides 63 and births 64. A similar situation occurred in 1980 and less obviously in 1929 and 1948.

Figure 5 was produced in the late 1980s, at the end of a very emotional, sixty-year period in Britain, so it is slightly out of phase with Figure 4a.

Our entry into the twenty first century has proved less-emotional: British birth and suicide figures are fairly steady (E&W births c700K; E&W suicides c3260), but:

UK Workers	1997	1998	1999	2000	2001	2002	2003
on strike (x1000)	130	93	141	183	180	943	151

During each period of crisis, high profile assassinations or violent political events occur. The destruction of New York's World Trade Centre on September 11th, 2001, was such an event. These happenings reveal a surge in anarchist or terrorist group emotion, expressed through the acts of one or more individuals.

A similar surge of emotion may affect the population as a whole, causing it to respond almost hysterically to the anarchist or terrorist incident: typically the world-wide personal awareness of President Kennedy's assassination in November 1963. However, it might be more accurate to say '*Kennedy was shot because I remember where I was at the time,*' rather than the reverse, because the speaker's awareness had probably been enhanced by the collective emotional surge.

The sunspot cycle seems to be the only astronomical phenomenon which matches the irregular, say seven to fifteen year, separation of the 'years of crises' and 'peak of prosperity'. Both events may be regarded, to a greater or lesser degree, as emotional turning points. Sunspots affect our weather. Once pressure for change has built up within a population, the change seems to be triggered by a sunspot-induced climatic extreme.

The Human Cycle

Let us travel with Britain as it struggles out of a depression, at C, and sets off around the cycle. After each crisis point and each zone, we will look back at history and, in some cases, recall a few words from the past which best illustrate the mood of the moment:

Figure 4b ZONE CD

Within this zone, economic pressure unites the nation. Groups must cooperate to survive. Realism, stoicism and nationalism predominate.

Nationalism can express itself as hostility to other nations: the more dire the depression; the greater the hostility.

After the severe mid-1930s depression, Britain was drawn into the 1939-45 Second World War.

Point D (the CRISIS OF SELF-ASSERTION*) At this point, increased confidence allows small pressure groups to break away from the nation, assert themselves and cause problems. There is a political swing to the

Left, as previously subjugated groups demand freedom and independence. Assassins are active. Suicides and births reach a peak. Climatic extremes are evident.

Author's note: * Each period of crisis has been given the name which best portrays the attitude of the population at that moment.

1947 - 48 *"A moment comes, which comes but rarely in history, when we step out from the old to the new, when an age ends and when the soul of a nation, long suppressed, finds utterance"* proclaimed Jawahar Nehru when India achieved its independence on the 14th August, 1947 [1]. Mahatma Gandhi was assassinated in January, 1948. In Britain, 1947 was the 4th wettest year on record (1979 was even wetter); January was the snowiest month for 150 years; February was the coldest month since records began in 1659.

Figure 4c ZONE DE

Confidence increases. Groups such as trade unions grow stronger. Ways of doing things (including political creed) pre-occupy the nation, which may question the validity of other creeds. Witch hunts and inquisitions occur. Prosperity continues to rise, as does the tempo of industrial unrest.

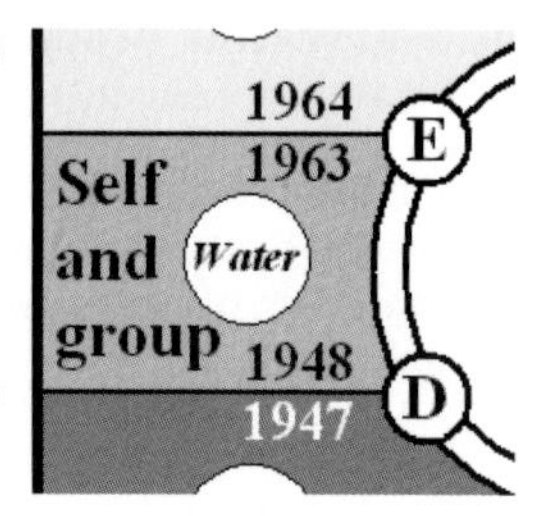

During the 1950s Britain suffered many crippling strikes in the docks, coal mines and motor industry. British forces fought in the 1950-53 Korean War, where several democracies successfully dammed the tide of communism with United Nations authority. In America, Senator McCarthy vehemently exposed people he believed to be communists.

Point E (the CRISIS OF SELF-RIGHTEOUSNESS) At this point, the buoyant economy elevates confidence and certainty to a higher level. The arts gain impetus. Pressure groups evaporate almost invisibly into very demanding, hedonistic, often rebellious individuals. Assassinations occur. There are sharp birth and suicide peaks, after an earlier surge of industrial disputes. There is extreme weather.

1963 – 64 US President Kennedy was assassinated on 22nd November, 1963. In the same year, London experienced the Big Freeze: the Thames froze over allowing the first car rally on ice; skaters were towed by cars; snow in London was two foot deep. Apart from the weather, passage through crisis point E was not particularly noticeable in UK, but emotion-related statistics recorded the moment (return to Figure 5). Sir Roy Strong [2] experienced the moment: "*1964 marked the crucial year of my life...I decided to be myself and everything just swam along. I wore broad ties, suits with flared trousers, high-vented jackets, Cuban heels, boldly patterned shirts from Ashers, a maxi-coat down to the ground. I copied my hats from Cecil Beaton.*" Sir Roy was not alone in his sartorial extremity: the hem of the mini-skirt would soon reach its highest point.

Author's note: I was prompted to look at emotion-related statistics by the very evident 'grouping' of assassinations in the mid-1960s: there were many in America at this time. Man is ubiquitous and the influences upon him are universal but, never the less, it is not easy to accurately date earlier occurrences of this crisis point.

Figure 4d ZONE EF

The nation exhibits great confidence and certainty. Hedonism abounds; the creative arts flourish; and feminism is more evident. The zone is characterised by determined individualism and self-righteousness, often to the point of inhumanity

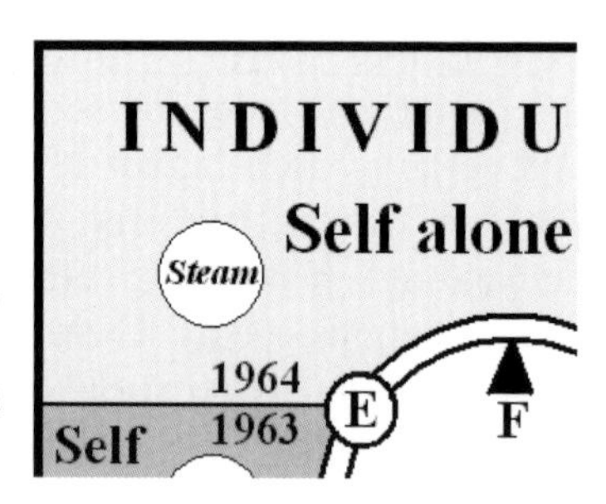

<u>During the 1960s</u>, Britain produced the Beatles and confident new styles appeared in almost every art form. In 1968, student violence flared up throughout Europe. Soon afterwards, Civil Rights marches started in Northern Ireland. In 1969, US forces in Vietnam reached their highest level (c700,000) but, by then, US resolve had been weakened by public response to the March 1968 My Lai incident [(3)].

Figure 4e ZONE FA

The situation worsens: extreme self-righteousness leads to moral laxity and corruption, while hedonism continues unabated.

Individuals continue to demand more money, despite the chaos their demands are causing.

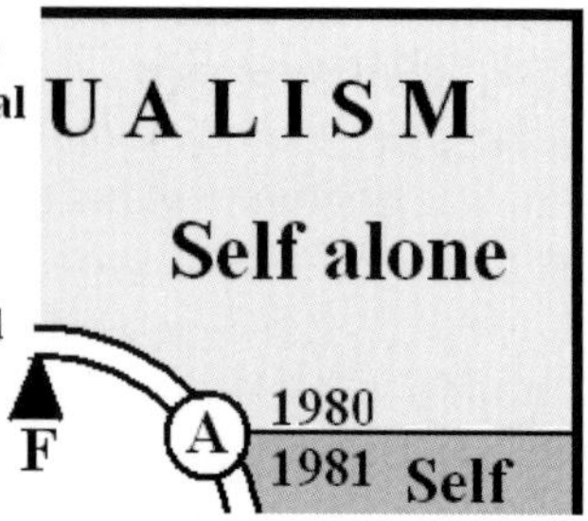

UALISM
Self alone
F
A
1980
1981
Self

<u>During the early 1970s</u>, striking miners brought down Britain's Conservative Government. The Labour government which followed was faced with hotly-contested 15% wage claims, dead left unburied, and

streets blocked by mountains of uncollected rubbish. Conditions worsened further until the Labour Government was eventually cast aside by its exasperated electorate.

Point A (the CRISIS OF DISILLUSIONMENT) The moment when sweets are withheld from a spoilt two-year old child: screams of rage, industrial riots and mob rule, as individuals unite to assault the government which, under pressure from the banks, is refusing to fund ever higher pay rises. Further regrouping occurs, as weaker, vulnerable individuals seek support. There are assassinations. There is a surge of compassion but a political swing to the Right. Emotion-related statistics peak, during a period of climatic extreme.

1979 Earl Mountbatten was assassinated. Britain was even wetter than it had been in 1947. 1980 America experienced a summer heat wave and drought which caused 10,000 deaths 1981 Hundreds of British women came together and encircled the Greenham Common US airbase, and Britain acquired a new leader, because: "*you know there are times, perhaps once every thirty years, when there is a sea change in politics. It does not matter what you do. There is a shift in what the public wants, and what it approves of. I suspect that there is now such a sea change - and it is for Margaret Thatcher*," said Jim Callaghan [4], her predecessor.

Author's note: Point A may merit a longer, perhaps three-year transition period (1979-1981).

Figure 4f ZONE AB

Individual and group disillusionment characterise this zone. There is irrational resentment of government, terrorism, anarchy, and continued social and industrial turmoil. Moral laxity and corruption linger within an extremely volatile, often irrational financial system. Nations struggle to avoid economic collapse amid violent torrents of emotion.

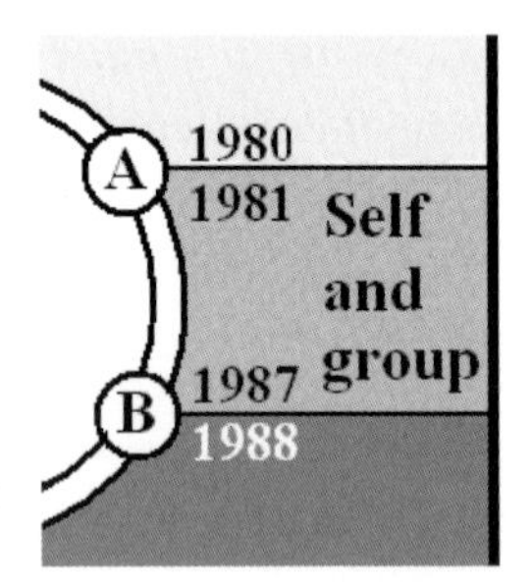

Throughout the 1980s, Britain was in turmoil. A better prepared British Conservative government faced up to the miners again and won, but only after a bitter struggle which scarred the nation. In contrast, popular musicians rallied to support Bob Geldof's 1985 Live Aid concert on behalf of Ethiopian famine victims: eight million pounds was raised in a few days.

Point B (the CRISIS OF REALISATION) At this point people are forced by circumstance to think more logically and recognise reality. The stock market crashes; house prices are threatened; fear drives groups closer together. Social turmoil either increases dramatically or begins to subside, dependent upon particular circumstance. Weather is extreme; there are assassinations and less obvious peaks in birth, suicide and 'workers on strike' statistics. Barriers may be assaulted and governments overthrown, but the number of striking workers normally decreases rapidly after this point.

1987 In October, Britain's stock market crashed and the Great Storm destroyed 15 million trees: it was the worst storm since 1703. In December, the Cold War effectively ended when the Reagan/Gorbachev INF treaty was signed. East European communism began to crumble and, in 1989, the Berlin Wall was torn down. 1988 A Pan Am Boeing 747 was blown up over Lockerbie: not an assassination, but an example of heightened group emotion bringing about a major terrorist incident.

Figure 4g ZONE BC

Continued rumblings of discontent, moderated by a growing acceptance of the need for national unity: the emergence of nationalism.

Productivity ceases to fall and then begins to rise: a prosperity rise will follow.

In earlier revolutions of the cycle, conditions in Zone BC often prompted migration ('Long Marches' and 'Great Treks') as groups banded together to seek salvation elsewhere.

Back at point C. As we reach this point, efficiency and productivity are starting to rise again; this leads eventually to rising prosperity. The human cycle enters its next revolution.

References:

(1) Jawahar Nehru's address to the nation reported in *End of Empire* Brian Lapping Granada Publishing 1985

(2) Sir Roy Strong: quoted in *Portrait of a Director under Fire.* Sunday Times Magazine, 1 June 1986 (Courtesy of THE SUNDAY TIMES newspaper)

(3) The My Lai incident took place on 16 March 1968: a large number of Vietnamese civilian men, women and children were callously murdered by US infantrymen. Suppressed at first, details of the horrific incident emerged months later to stun the American people.

(4) Jim Callaghan: reported in Sunday Times, May 1987

6. THE VIOLENCE CYCLE

Photograph 6 Plaque set into a Manchester dockside paving slab

The sombre words on this dockside plaque remind us that man's journey around the long cycle leaves its mark on the landscape. The journey also leaves an imprint in his mind and "*traumatic memories do not wear away normally but remain an active and* <u>*unconscious*</u> *force motivating behaviour*" (Freud & Breuer [1]). It is this unconscious force, fashioned at one point and exercised at another, which links together the violence cycle.

Cheer up!

Before you read this section, please be aware that action can be taken to minimise the build up of inflammatory forces within a nation. Individual violence, revolution and war are largely predictable but not inevitable. Prevention is difficult: sea changes in attitude, outlook and behaviour are called for. We have already noted that Switzerland successfully avoids war: the epilogue of this book offers Britain a war avoidance strategy.

Violence

The term violence is vague: let us assume we mean *aggressive tendencies in the individual* and *propensity to engage in war in the nation.* Assaults, rape and murder result from the former; wars from the latter. The individual combatants in a war may not be aggressive, but their nations may have a high propensity to engage in conflict or war. For the moment, to simplify matters, we will call the outcomes of individual, group and national aggression 'violence'. Further on, we will be more precise.

The violence cycle

Figure 6 is a very simple portrayal of the violence cycle. The nature of individual violence will vary around the cycle. Similarly, the prime motivator of a long war may evolve as the passage of time carries that war out of one zone into the next.

If you look at the night sky, you see very many stars; if you look at history, you see very many wars. We understand how some stars relate to our world; this section relates some exemplary British, European and American wars to the violence cycle. After absorbing this section, the reader may wish to relate other wars or violent uprisings to the cycle.

Figure 6 THE VIOLENCE CYCLE

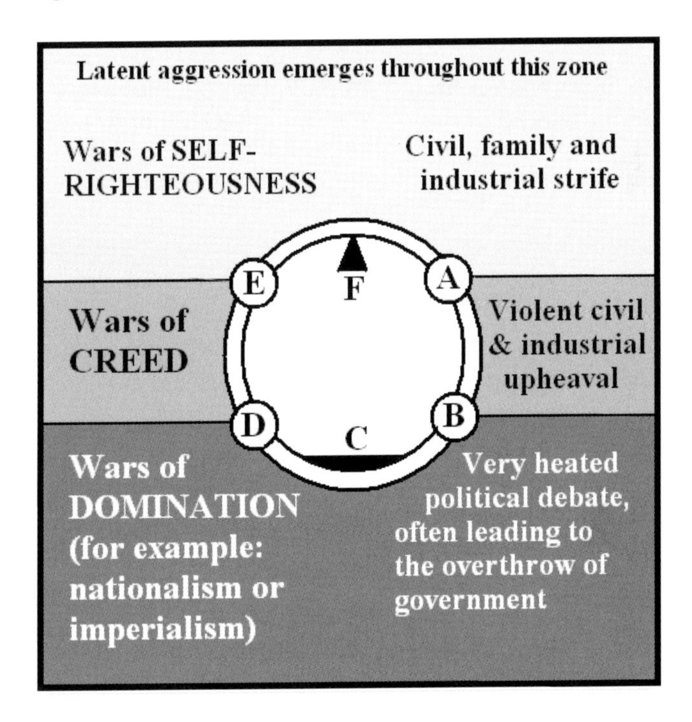

The violence cycle is best understood by addressing the following questions:

a. What is the significance of the crisis points (A, B, D and E)?

b. How is violence generated within the cycle?

c. How do the three categories of war differ?

The crisis points

By looking at history, listening to voices from the past and examining emotion-related statistics, we might place the crisis points in the following two-year brackets:

A.	Disillusionment	1876-77, 1919-20, 1980-81
B	Realisation	1884-85, 1929-30, 1987-88
D	Self-assertion	1903-04, 1947-48, 2001-02
E	Self-righteousness	1908-09, 1963-64, (c2015?)

Imagine a stone caught in a car tyre. As the tyre rotates, the stone scrapes the hard road causing a succession of sparks. If there were four stones caught about the circumference of the tyre, there would be a quadrupled succession of sparks. The crisis points are the stones on the tyre; the sparks may ignite revolution or war.

Put in the simplest terms: sudden adversity at A lights a fuse, which may provoke a minor war; when the fuse burns down to B, it ignites the dynamite of revolution; at D the invigorated, freshly-governed nation experiences an attitude change causing it to question other nations' creeds; at E it experiences a further attitude change, becomes irrational, and may wage war relentlessly against anyone after the slightest provocation.

The French Revolution and the Napoleonic Wars which followed offer one example of the process. Look carefully, and you will see the same pattern emerging, less violently, in Britain today: after the turbulent 1980s, the Conservative government was overthrown (albeit democratically); the new, excitable, radical Labour government encouraged by an American government just jolted by the 9/11 incident (point D), entered the second Gulf War.

The generation of violence

The author's dictionary describes violence as "*behaviour that is intended to hurt others physically*", and aggression as "*angry or threatening behaviour or feelings that often result in fighting*". Violence stems from aggression but where do these *feelings that often result in fighting* come from? Man is probably born with some aggression; without it he would not have evolved. Furthermore, a predisposition toward aggression may be forged during childhood or early adulthood. External causes can awaken this aggression: jealousy, perceived deprivation, ill-treatment, and even noise while one is trying to concentrate.

If we look at the behaviour of Britain's 'atomised' population in the late 1960s/early 1970s (zone EF) we see "*apparently motiveless aggression against persons or property - battered wives and babies, hooliganism, vandalism, mugging and communal violence on the football terrace or strike picket line - often motivated, it would appear, by nothing more than an antagonism against society as a whole*" said the Chief Inspector of Constabulary [(3)] in1972. Interestingly, during an equivalent period in the 1860s, when Britain was, again, remote from major war, 'violence against the person' incidents climbed steadily from 1860 to 1865: almost exactly the duration of the American Civil War.

What caused the violence in the late 1960s/early 1970s? Britain's post-war generations, which were making most of the noise, had 'never-had-it-so-good' according to British Prime Minister Harold Macmillan. The main cause seemed to be *perceived deprivation*. If you tell men in blue suits that the men in green suits are getting all the goodies, the men in blue suits get angry; if you say men are getting all the goodies, women get angry; if you say everyone is entitled to cheese and cheese runs out, everyone gets angry. Perceived deprivation was also identified as the cause of communal violence in USA during the1970s. A US Government Commission on the Causes and Prevention of Violence [(4)] noted that "*the greater the deprivation the individual perceives relative to his expectation, the greater his discontent; the more widespread and intense the discontent, the more likely and severe is the civil strife*".

Point A may be regarded as the beginning of each successive violence cycle. Man experiences a host of stimuli as he travels around the cycle: some of which sow the seeds of aggression while others prompt its release. At Point A, the *crisis of disillusionment*, several generations begin to violently release their aggression, while younger, impressionable generations absorb its influence. If a major war occurred earlier, in zone EF, this aggression is subdued; if not, the aggression is fierce. Most recently, from the late 1970s through to the early 1990s, we saw screams of rage; rebellion; fisticuffs; rock throwing; abuse and vitriolic hatred, as major segments of the British workforce assailed the government.

Why did this British aggression linger into the 1980s? Why wasn't there a war during the earlier 1964/73 period? The short answer: Britain and Europe were firmly in the hands of an older generation who had been well and truly inoculated against war. Let us now examine this inoculation: the First World War, the Second World War and the Korean War.

The First World War (WW1)

WW1 occurred in the top band of rising prosperity. It appears on Figure 7a with the other major *wars of self-righteousness.*

Figure 7a THE PATTERN OF WAR DURING FOUR PERIODS OF RISING PROSPERITY

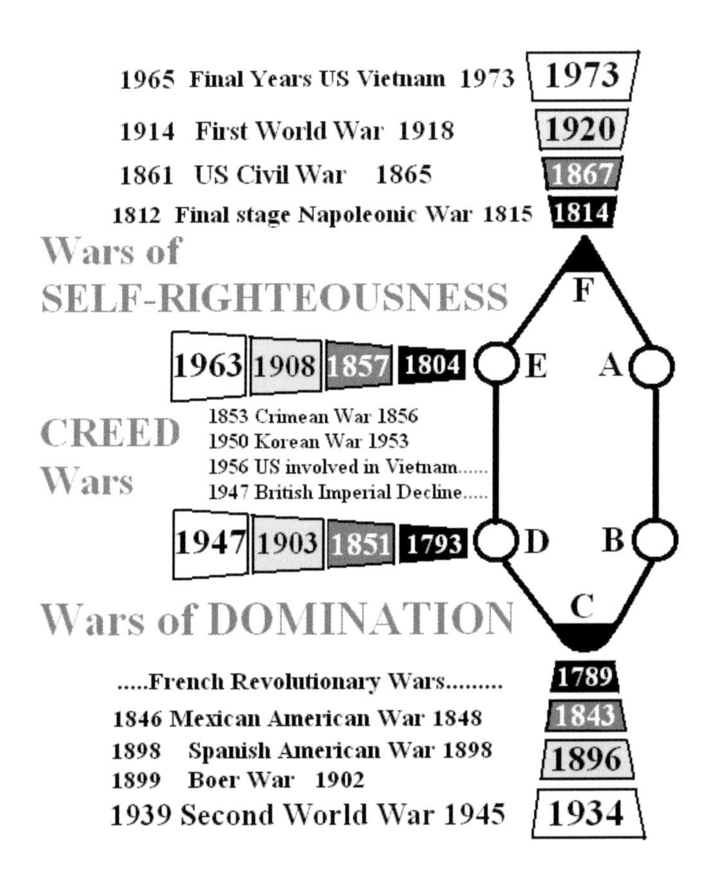

During early 1914, the main European powers were confident and competitive, but they were not overtly aggressive. A minor incident which called into play

several complex military alliances drew the great powers into WW1. Each nation believed itself to be in the right: particularly the main aggressor, Germany, which saw itself dangerously hemmed in by France and Russia.

In essence, European states, particularly Britain and Germany, were rich and powerful, and there was a naval arms race; Russia and France were in an alliance which straddled and threatened Germany; the German response was a defence plan which said, in essence, *at the first sign of trouble, we beat France (by going through Belgium), and then we beat Russia*; Britain was allied to Belgium, and had an informal naval agreement with France (in return for the French fleet guarding the Mediterranean, the British fleet would guard the Channel and the French ports); these and other military alliances became enmeshed in the Balkans.

A precarious balance of power prevailed until a student shot Archduke Ferdinand and his Duchess in Sarajevo, on June 28th, 1914. A fuse was lit; the burning fuse snaked through the numerous European military alliances, starting fires, until Europe was ablaze with war. Few of the soldiers involved really understood what they were fighting for, but each of the governments involved *strongly believed that they were in the right* (even the British government, which was supported and then led by the ardent pacifist David Lloyd-George). Historians and writers have exhaustively examined WW1 to establish its cause but, concealed within the maze of information produced, we see a classic w*ar of self-righteousness*.

At first, British men flocked eagerly to the recruiting stations *to help the poor Belgians*; not so in later years, when conscription became necessary. Once WW1 had started, there seemed no honourable way to stop it; the killing continued until the participants were exhausted. Britain and her allies won, but only just: the flower of British manhood perished; the British Empire was impoverished; the Low Countries were devastated and Russia experienced a revolution. The Ottoman and Austro-Hungarian empires were completely destroyed and the defeated Germans were penalised to the point of simmering resentment. WW2 would follow.

Figure 7b TOP BAND WARS

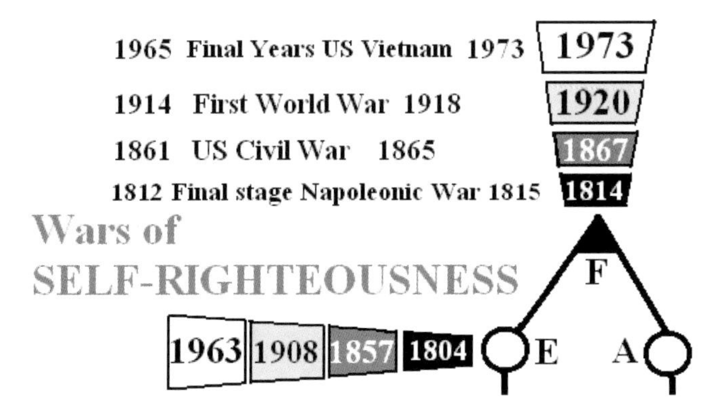

Other top band wars

The latter phases of both the Napoleonic Wars and the US Vietnam War were prolonged by the messianic self-righteousness of Napoleon and the United States government respectively. During the American Civil War the attitude of both sides was very self-righteous, particularly that of the Southern States, reported here by Ulysses S Grant [(5)] "*... the Southern slave owners believed that, in some way, the ownership of slaves conferred a sort of patent of nobility - a right to govern independent of the interest or wishes of those who did* *not hold such property. They convinced themselves, first, of the divine origins of the institution and, next, that that particular institution was not safe in the hands of any body of legislators but themselves."* The fuse of the American Civil War was lit many years earlier, in 1856, when very self-righteous proslavery hot-heads clashed violently with antislavery hot-heads (John Brown et al) in Kansas.

The Second World War (WW2)

WW2 occurred in the bottom band of rising prosperity. It appears with other major *wars of domination* at the base of Figure 7a and on Figure 7c.

Figure 7c BOTTOM BAND WAR

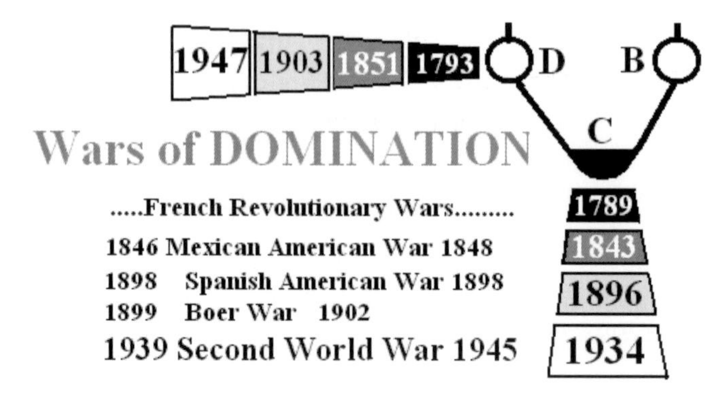

WW2 was, quite clearly, a war of domination: Adolf Hitler wished to create a 1000-year Reich; he had begun to swallow-up weaker nations before Britain became involved. Hitler's malevolent character was forged by the cycle: his abusive father died when he was thirteen; his mother a few years later. After years as a drifter Hitler served throughout WW1 in some of the worst battles [(6)]. He took no leave and received no letters, but he was twice decorated for bravery and rose to the rank of corporal. After that searing experience and the sacrifice of two million of his comrades, the news of Germany's surrender moved Hitler to tears: tears which would soon turn to rage. Hitler was not alone: many had been seared; many had been humiliated. German resentment simmered; Hitler rose to power; the rest is history.

Other wars of domination. Ulysses S Grant (5) fought in the Mexican American War (1846-48) and said of it: "*It was an instance of a republic following the bad example of European monarchies in not considering justice in their desire to acquire additional territory.*" America acquired more territory during the later Spanish-American War of 1898, albeit after some Spanish provocation. Civil rights, gold, diamonds and religion influenced the Boer War (1899-1902) but, in the end, Britain's imperial power was exercised in South Africa, despite fierce opposition from David Lloyd-George and many other public figures.

The Korean War

The Korean War occurred in the centre band of rising prosperity. It is shown on Figure 7a and Figure 7d with other *creed wars*.

The Korean War (1950-53) followed closely behind WW2, during which the Japanese occupied South Korea. When the Japanese withdrew, power fell into the hands of a weak, American-backed despot threatened by his more powerful communist neighbour, North Korea. After WW2, communist encroachment in Europe had alarmed Britain and America, who viewed the North Korean attack on South Korea in June 1950 in this light. The absence of Russia from a Security Council vote allowed USA and its allies to bring about the despatch of a United Nations force to Korea to repel the invaders. The prime motivation for the war appears to have been a desire to stem the communist tide which was slowly enveloping large areas of the Far East.

Creed has been chosen as the best single word to categorize the centre band wars, but it should be read in the broad political sense. In zone DE, we find wars about 'ways of doing things': particularly methods of government or the cultural, rather than belief aspects of religion.

Figure 7d WARS IN THE CENTRE BAND

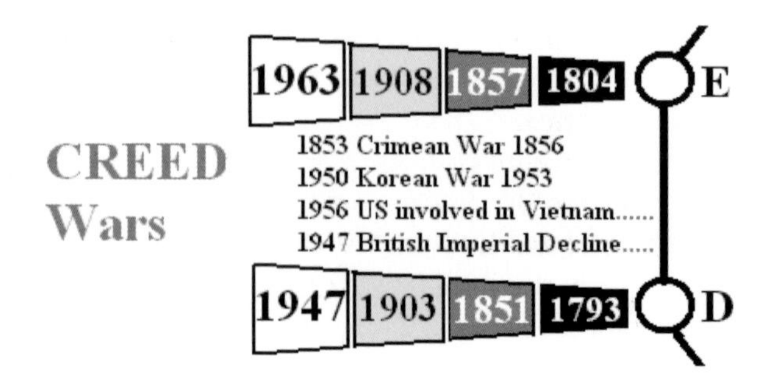

The recent Second Gulf War has proved controversial: the initial justification (removal of Saddam Hussein's weapons of mass destruction) quickly evolved into 'regime change' (the need to impose democracy). This war could reasonably be placed between D and E, had the next turn of the cycle been shown. The occupying forces of America and Britain are facing considerable resistance because, at this point in time, many Iraqis feel very strongly about *their* culture and *their* way of doing things. We will examine the reason for this strong cultural motivation in a later section.

For reasons which will be explained in the next section, fewer wars occur in the centre band. Those that do occur are not always tidy in their gestation. The Crimean War (1853-56) had its roots in a dispute between two sects of monks over the keys of a monastery in Jerusalem; after that, everyone seemed to join in: Russia, Turkey, Britain, France, et al. When the war ended, everyone met in Paris, shook hands like gentlemen, and agreed to restore their original borders; they also agreed to open the Black Sea and Lower Danube to the merchant fleets of all countries.

The US Vietnam War was rooted in the centre band. After losing the bitter, post-WW2 conflict in Indochina, France pulled out in 1954, leaving the area divided into communist North Vietnam and South Vietnam. In 1956, hundreds of American advisers moved in to help South Vietnam hold back a second communist tide (after Korea). During the years which followed, the conflict grew into what seemed, to many outsiders, a liberation struggle on the part of the Vietnamese against a new occupying force. To the 1950s American government, driven by the illusory concept of 'freedom', it was a quasi-crusade; in the late 1960s it became a crusade but the communist devil won. The American government was humiliated; many of America's younger generation were traumatised.

After WW2, the British Empire entered its final phase. Until 1947, Britain had ruled more land and people than any government in history. During the three decades between India's independence in 1947 and Southern Rhodesia's in 1980, the British Empire shed most of its territories [(7)]. The rundown of empire was sometimes graceful but often violent; British servicemen have been killed on duty in every year since the end of WW2, except 1968: the year students rampaged through the capitals of Europe. It's a strange world.

Hopefully, we now understand *when* the three types of war occur. The next section will explain *why* they occur.

References:

(1) *Studies in Hysteria* Freud and Breuer 1895

(2) *The Future of Violence* Gerald Priestland, Hamish Hamilton 1974, including the quotations attributed to:

(3) Report of the Chief Inspector of Constabulary 1972

(4) US Government Commission on the Causes and Prevention of Violence.

(5) *Personal Memoirs* Ulysses S Grant Charles L Webster 1885

(6) *Rise and Fall of the Third Reich* William L Shirer Book Club Associates 1972.

(7) *End of Empire* Brian Lapping Granada Publishing 1985

7. WHY WAR?

Photograph 7 Londoners crossing the Millennium Bridge

The violence cycle tells us when each type of war is likely to occur. In this section we explain why each type of war occurs.

Crowds

When a person is one member of an unassociated group (for example, five people who have just alighted from a bus) that person is likely to behave and react in the same way as he or she would in isolation. However, if that person is one of five people struggling to get on a crowded bus, he or she would behave and react very differently because the group has become what is known as a *psychological crowd*: a group of seemingly unassociated individuals united by circumstance.

A psychological crowd exhibits one very significant characteristic: the intellect of each individual within that crowd is weakened and unconscious forces within the minds of crowd members gain the upper hand [(1)]. These are the same unconscious forces we noted in the last chapter: they are the result of cultural influence and each person's circumstance during his or her formative years. A simple example: during military service in the early 1960s, the author noted that English people queued patiently but Germans tended to jump the queue. When he asked each nationality, in turn, why they behaved in the way they did, they gave the same answer: it was because of wartime food shortages!

A nation may be viewed as a large crowd. Pressured by circumstance, it becomes a psychological crowd and "*whoever be the individuals that compose it, however like or unlike their mode of life, their occupations, their character, or their intelligence, the fact that they have been transformed into a crowd puts them into the possession of a sort of collective mind which makes them think, feel and act in manner quite different from that in which each individual of them would think, feel, and act were he in a state of isolation*", explained Gustave Le Bon [(1)] in 1896. The underlining within this quotation has been added for emphasis.

To understand why the pattern of warfare occurs, we have to understand what is happening within a nation's collective mind as it experiences the long cycle. In particular, we need to look at the variation of its state of mind. Once we have done this, we can use a psychologist's tool, *transactional analysis*, to partially explain the pattern of warfare. The next section will provide the final piece of the jigsaw.

A very brief introduction to transactional analysis [(2)]

When we converse with our parents, children, colleagues or friends, we subconsciously adopt one of the three negotiator levels:

PARENT: to impose our will upon the other person(s).

ADULT: to reason with them, or talk to them as an equal.

CHILD: to display subservience; or to experience (or express) delight, pleasure, or dismay.

At work, our boss might adopt the ADULT level if he wishes to discuss something with us. If he wants something done without fail, he would probably adopt the PARENT level. The boss's secretary might normally adopt the ADULT level in her dealings with him. If she is having trouble with her computer, she might adopt the CHILD level to encourage his assistance.

People's minds flip up and down through the various levels from one moment to the next. Successful human relationships depend upon this mental agility. A relationship problem occurs when a person's mind is locked in, or out of, one of the negotiator levels, due to childhood trauma or an unduly severe, or unduly lax upbringing. If the person is locked in the PARENT level, he or she is very likely to fall out with a parental boss. If he or she is locked in the CHILD level, he or she may be very creative but might not be trustworthy. If he or she is locked out of the CHILD level, he or she might never experience love.

Figure 8 THE STATES OF MIND OF TWO NATIONS AS TIME CARRIES THEM AROUND THE LONG CYCLE

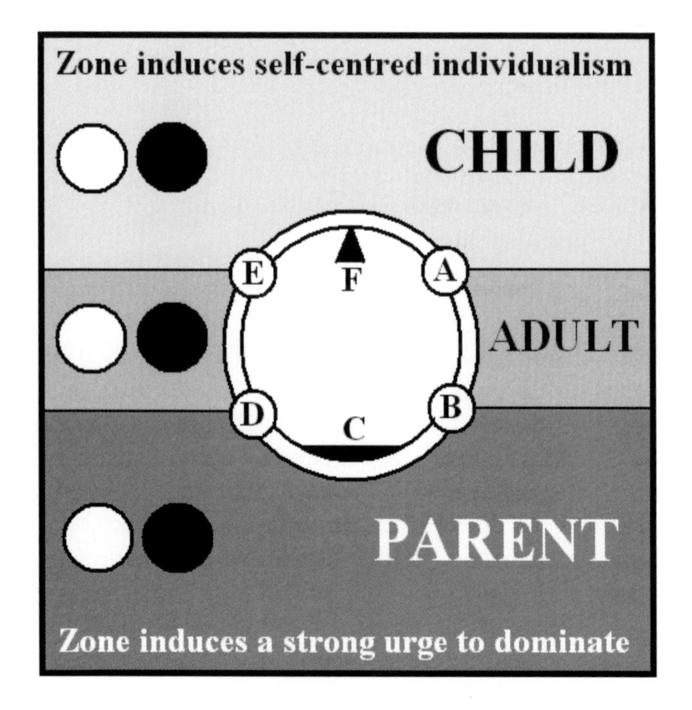

The relationship of nations

Looking at Figure 8, we see that SELF AND NATION, SELF AND GROUP and SELF ALONE have become PARENT, ADULT, and CHILD: that is, the three negotiator levels. Why is this so? Short answer: the circumstances in each band.

POPULATION STATE	*Circumstances*	*NEGOTIATOR LEVEL*
SELF & NATION	Nationalism Urge to dominate	PARENT
SELF & GROUP	Diminished nationalism Restrained individualism	ADULT
SELF ALONE	Rampant individualism Self-righteousness	CHILD

As the two, black and white nations shown on the figure journey around the long cycle, linked by the global economy, they circulate together through the three bands. Within each successive band, both nations are locked by prevailing circumstances into one particular negotiator level. Consequently, as the two nations begin to rise from the depth of depression, they adopt the following sequence of joint negotiator levels:

Zone CD PARENT-PARENT)
Zone DE ADULT-ADULT) in rising prosperity
Zone EF CHILD-CHILD)

Zone FA CHILD-CHILD)
Zone AB ADULT-ADULT) in falling prosperity
Zone BC PARENT-PARENT)

For the moment, we can ignore the three falling prosperity zones. War is normally subdued in these zones; the next section will explain why.

The sequence reveals why wars of domination occur in zone CD; fewer, milder wars occur in the zone DE; and wars of childish self-righteousness occur in zone EF. Like school playground fights, the latter wars are usually caused by irreconcilable argument over a rights issue, or the irrational escalation of a minor incident.

While all wars are destructive, wars of self-righteousness tend to be the most lethal. The next section will explain why, as we look more deeply into the nation's mind.

References:

(1) *The Crowd: a study of the popular mind*
Book I Chapter I   Gustave Le Bon, 1896

This book may be viewed on the internet:
http://etext.virginia.edu/toc/modeng/public/BonCrow.htm

(2) The following works of Eric Berne MD:

Games People Play   Penguin 1964
Sex in Human Loving   Penguin 1970

TRANSACTIONAL ANALYSIS Internet link:
http://www.businessballs.com/transact.htm

8. IN THE MIND

Photograph 8 Children meeting the Burger King in Huntsville, Alabama

Transactional analysis helped us to understand why three different types of war occurred during rising prosperity. To explain why similar wars do not occur during falling prosperity, we have to look more deeply into the collective mind of the nation: in particular, we have to look at *psychopathy* and *obsession.* Just as transactional analysis helps us to understand how human beings relate to each other, these two intangible concepts, psychopathy and obsession, help us to understand human motivation and behaviour.

When we use the word *psychopathy*, it means '*the qualities or characteristics of a psychopath*', just as *obsession* means '*the qualities or characteristics of an obsessive'*. Both psychopathy and obsession have frightening connotations, but both are present within all our minds to a greater or lesser degree.

Psychopathy

Psychiatrists tell us that psychopathy relates closely to *certainty*. A *psychopath* is certain, decisive and unconstrained by guilt, however bad the outcome of his actions. Psychopathy is a childish quality: a young child might pull the wings off a butterfly without realising the suffering it is inflicting, whereas a normal adult would experience guilt.

Adult psychopathy arises when the normal development of a child's mind is constrained: for example, by cruelty or a severe emotional shock. We might say that Nature builds a shell around the mind of a trauma-stricken child to keep out the horror the child is experiencing. When the child grows up, this shell remains in place and it shields that person from guilt when he or she commits a horrifying act.

Psychopathy is essentially a guilt barrier between a person's mind and his or her actions or environment. It may be a thick or a thin barrier, dependent upon the degree of trauma experienced by the child. Consequently, the adult psychopathy spectrum might extend from a mild insensitivity to the feelings of others, to the axe-wielding, maniacal behaviour of the infamous Charles Manson.

Crowd influences

If the mood of a nation is cheerful, cheerful individuals gain confidence; if a nation is mournful, cheerful people are likely to be subdued. We might say, therefore, that the mental traits of a nation amplify matching mental traits within its individuals. In particular, we might deduce that a high psychopathy level within a nation's collective mind will encourage a psychopath to commit an atrocity. As we shall see shortly, this seems to be the case. More controversially, the high level of psychopathy within the national mind could exist as an unconscious force influencing the whole of the national (psychological) crowd. This could give rise to the *death wish* which Freud offered as an explanation for the high level of casualties in the First World War. This may seem a bit far fetched: Nature, alone, knows what is really happening.

Viewed externally, from afar (for example, by British people observing the latter stages of the Vietnam War), psychopathy seems to exist within a nation's collective mind as a guilt barrier (and, to a certain extent, a pain barrier) between those older, self-righteous generations whose certainty promotes a war and the younger, less powerful generations enduring that war.

Gauging the national mood

To understand and assess the mental state of a nation as it journeys around the long cycle, we need to examine its ever-changing view of life. It is this 'view of life' which will motivate the nation and govern its mind at each point. To understand what we mean, imagine yourself in a casino: every turn of the dice falls to your advantage and you win a million pounds. On your way home, at an almost deserted but blind road junction, the traffic light suddenly turns to amber. What do you do: apply the brakes, or accelerate? Still feeling lucky, you might well accelerate. If you had been less fortunate at the casino, you would probably apply the brakes. This is a simple example of the influence of external events on the mind.

The influence of events is likely to be strongest at the *crisis points* A, B, D and E: the four points where the nation seems to experience a great surge of emotion. Figure 9 portrays what the nation sees during each of those surges:

Figure 9 THE VIEW OF LIFE SEEN BY A NATION AS IT TRAVELS AROUND THE LONG CYCLE

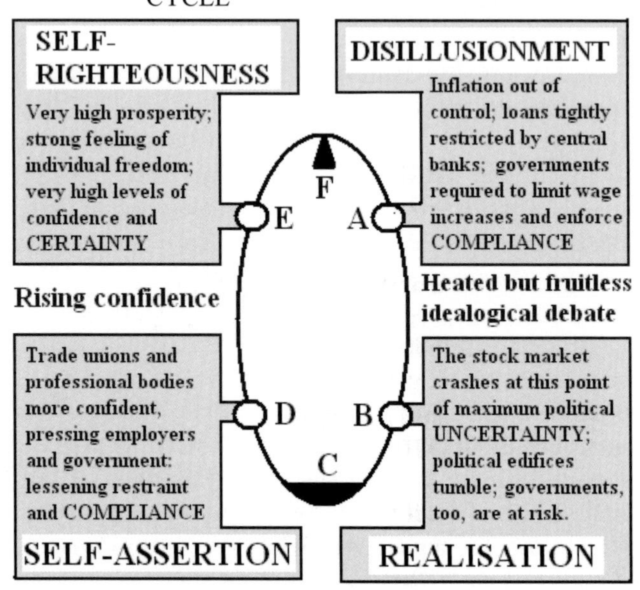

We might reasonably assume that, if rising prosperity amplifies a particular human quality, falling prosperity will attenuate it. For example: as prosperity rises, people become more independent; as it falls, they regroup. Similarly, if we know at which point on the cycle a particular quality maximises or minimises, we should be able to plot a chart showing, very roughly, how that quality varies about the cycle. To illustrate what we mean, let us look first at psychopathy.

Looking at Figure 9, we see that CERTAINTY appears to maximise at Point E the *crisis of self-righteousness,* and minimise at Point B, the *crisis of realisation,* after years of fruitless ideological debate. Beyond Point B, events like the stock market crash increase certainty: they enable deep seated but irrational views to be forcefully challenged and, by the time Point C has been reached, prolonged but converging political argument will have achieved a more certain consensus. Using the maximum certainty and minimum certainty points, we can produce Figure 10:

Figure 10 THE VARIATION OF PSYCHOPATHY AROUND THE LONG CYCLE

Psychopathy (characterised by CERTAINTY) rises at a steady rate from its MINUMUM (dark grey) level at Point B, until it reaches its MAXIMUM (dark grey) level at Point E; beyond E, it declines at the same rate until Point B is reached.

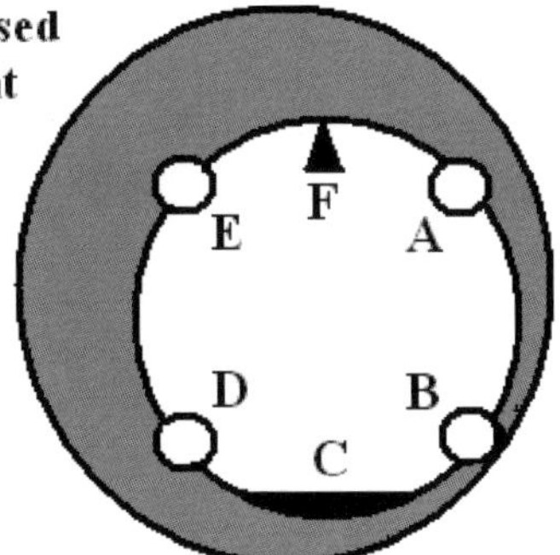

The presence of a high level of psychopathy within the collective mind of a nation will allow that nation to hurl its subjects into the flames of war without any collective feelings of guilt: "*In our last draft was a man who had been invalided out of the Navy with shock after being torpedoed four times: conscripted into the Army in Category C3, he was reclassified A and sent here,*" reported Captain J C Dunn [(1)], Medical Officer of the 2nd Battalion Royal Welch Fusiliers, from the trenches in Flanders in June 1917. An officer colleague of Captain Dunn was so appalled by the emotional detachment of those at home in England, that he was glad to return to the comradeship in the trenches.

Apart from grieving relatives and those directly involved, most older-generation Britons continued to promote the First World War as a laudable but detached patriotic venture. This view was maintained, even after the war, when Luton town council organised a Peace Dinner but omitted to invite any ex-servicemen. Hundreds of aggrieved veterans, many of whom were unemployed, rioted; set fire to the town hall; dragged a piano into the street and sang a rousing chorus of their old wartime favourite: *Keep the home fires burning*! [(2)]

In 1963 (at Point E) the Myra Hindley/Ian Bradley Moors Murders occurred in Britain; in 1968, the My Lai episode occurred in Vietnam; in 1969, the Charles Manson killings occurred in California. Each incident fell within the high psychopathy region EF.

Psychopathy seems to be a product of affluence. It may be Nature's way of limiting the population of rich nations. Rich nations are prone to hedonism and lax morality; both destroy the family; children are physically and emotionally damaged; the overall level of psychopathy rises.

Obsession

While psychopathy might be said to be wealth related, obsession appears to be culture related. Obsession seems to be Nature's way of breaking down the sandcastles created by the more industrious nations. Psychiatrists tell us that obsession's beneficial qualities (*scrupulosity, reliability, self control and honesty*) are the prerequisites of efficient production, but obsession brings with it malevolent qualities (*compliance and ritual to the point of idiocy, immorality or inhumanity; plus a strong urge to dominate*).

In this section, *scrupulosity, reliability, self-control and honesty* are banded together so that they can be considered as a single trait: *compliance.*

If we look at Figure 9 and remember the human cycle we can see that the increasingly feckless, self-centred population receives its first jolt at Point A, the *crisis of disillusionment*. Laxity is no longer tolerated, accounting becomes more precise and greater industrial efficiency is demanded by the banks which control lending. We might assume, therefore, that compliance minimises at Point A. After Point A, circumstances force compliance to rise until Point D. At Point D, the *crisis of self-assertion*, trade unions and other reactionary groups begin to re-assert themselves, thus attenuating the dedication and compliance of their members. We might assume, therefore, that compliance is maximum at Point D. Using these minimum compliance and maximum compliance points, we can produce Figure 11:

Figure 11 THE VARIATION OF OBSESSION AROUND THE LONG CYCLE

Obsession (characterised by COMPLIANCE) rises at a steady rate from its MINIMUM (light grey) level at Point A, until it reaches its MAXIMUM (light grey) level at Point D; beyond D, it declines at the same rate until Point A is reached.

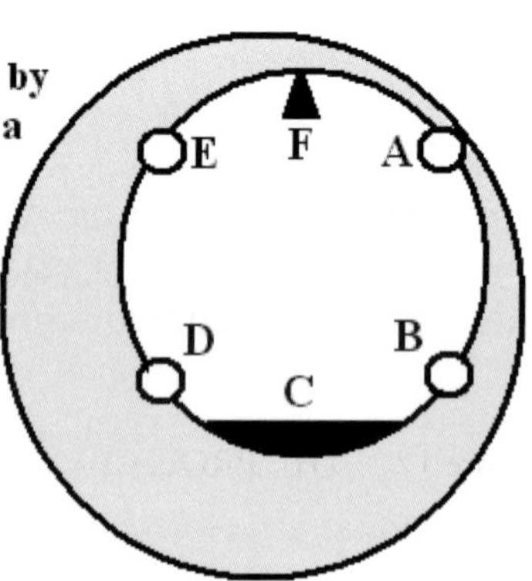

The latest *crisis of self-assertion*, Point D, probably occurred during 2001-2002; consequently, obsession was still at a high level in 2006. Fifty people were killed by terrorist bombs in Delhi as this page was being written: the latest in a series of loud bangs which has unsettled national governments preoccupied with their illusory *war on terror*. While psychopathy shields the mind from guilt, obsession (compliance and ritual to the point of inhumanity, plus a strong urge to dominate) negates guilt and motivates the terrorist.

Obsession was high in 1945, at the end of the Second World War. This is evident from a description of German concentration camp staff by D C Comper [(3)], a WW2 war crimes investigator: *"...all but a very few cases had no feeling of guilt because they had merely been obeying orders. Until we got used to this we found this attitude utterly breathtaking, best personified by the Camp Commandant of Sachsenhausen who complained bitterly to his interrogators that his gas chambers were much too small to maintain his quota and Berlin had persistently refused to do anything for him.*"

<u>The probability of war</u>

If we add the varying level of obsession to that of psychopathy, we arrive at Figure 12 (a very rough guide to the probability of war):

Figure 12 THE PROBABILITY OF WAR

Conclusions

Figure 10 seems to confirm the transactional analysis explanation for the cause of war in the top band: *certainty.* Figure 11 seems to confirm the cause of war in the bottom band: *dominance.* We might expect this because the three intangible concepts - transactional analysis, psychopathy and obsession - each try to fathom the same deeper levels of the mind. Figures 10 and 11 do not indicate why fewer wars occur in zone DE but the high level of obsession at the start of zone DE (see Figure 11) explains the *creed, or way of doing things,* cause of the wars that do occur.

Figures 10 and 11 suggest that both psychopathy and obsession are higher, cumulatively, during the rise in prosperity than they are during its fall. When we add the psychopathy level to the obsession level (Figure 12) the difference between rising prosperity and falling prosperity is accentuated, and we can see why most major wars occur during rising prosperity.

References:

(1) *The War the Infantry Knew 1914-19*
Capt J C Dunn PS King Ltd 1938
(Courtesy of the Royal Welch Fusiliers Regimental Museum)

(2) Recounted in an episode of *Not Forgotten*,
(Channel 4 TV series about WW1 memorials)

(3) *Who were the real Nazis?* D C Comper
Letter, London Standard March 1987

(4) *The Art of Psychotherapy* Anthony Storr
Secker and Warburg/Heinmann 1974

Epilogue

We think too small, like the frog at the bottom of the well. He thinks the sky is only as big as the top of the well. If he surfaced, he would have an entirely different view.

Mao Tse-Tung

Many people are aware of the long cycle and the pattern of war. Fewer people are aware of the human cycle and the solar influences which govern it; even fewer understand how all four phenomena relate to each other. I have tried to raise that level of understanding.

War avoidance

War avoidance would seem impossible for an imperial power, or for a nation allied to other nations to such an extent that, together, they constitute an imperial power. Throughout history, Nature has been the destroyer of proud empires; war has provided the means. Empires are beset by war during both their expansion and their decline, but it is possible for a peaceful nation to emerge from the ashes of empire. For this to happen, that nation must declare its independence, shed all imperial pretensions, terminate all military alliances, set up a credible self-defence organisation and consistently maintain a moderate level of prosperity.

Looking back

Two decades ago, I set out to investigate and explain the relationship between the long cycle and war, which Kondratieff had pointed out in his research paper. After completing my research, I anticipated that 2002 might be the next *crisis of self-assertion*; that Irish terrorism would temporarily decline; that Britain might go to war before 2002 and that Britain would remain at peace between 2002 and 2015. Britain's forces are still engaged in the Middle East but my other three predictions have proved correct.

Looking around

Religious conflict troubles the world: a strong faith engenders certainty; certainty allows people to commit violence without guilt. If one adds a heightened level of obsession, one sees the present Israeli-Palestinian unrest, religious militancy in Iran and world-wide Muslim terrorism.

Soldiers from America and its allies are occupying Iraq and Afghanistan, as part of the illusory *war on terror.* Unsettled, in 2006, by a maelstrom of lethal violence but honour bound to continue, the allied governments struggle to introduce costly, sophisticated methods of government into two barren, emotion-racked regions where religion and tribal loyalty have reigned for centuries: their brave soldiers suffer the consequences.

Looking ahead

As obsession declines and psychopathy rises, the nature of violence will change: certainty will overtake dominance as the prime motivator. A sudden, steep escalation of public and private sector pay disputes will herald the arrival of the next *crisis of self-righteousness.* This is likely to occur around 2015 and be prompted by sunspot cycle 24 (http://www.sec.noaa.gov/SolarCycle).

Assassinations or major terrorist atrocities may occur. The weather will probably be extreme. If there is no immediate social disturbance, a period of calm will follow, akin to the years 1964 to 1968; after this, widespread violence is likely to erupt suddenly, often spontaneously, throughout the world.

If this seems incredible, look back at 1968: violent student demonstrations shook many European and North American cities; thousands of Russian troops ruthlessly re-introduced Soviet control in Czechoslovakia; a sudden, fierce Vietcong *Tet* offensive intensified the war in Vietnam; the brutal stage of the *Cultural Revolution* raged throughout China and, in the Middle East, smoke was still rising from the 1967 Arab-Israeli *Six-Day War*. If you are still not convinced that violence can occur simultaneously around the world, look at the years 1909-1914.

Beyond 2015, Britain will probably experience social unrest due to *perceived deprivation* (see pages 39 and 40). This problem may be worse than it was in the late 1960s/early 1970s because Britain's new multicultural society is likely to spawn a broader spectrum of perceived deprivation; furthermore, many English people may still feel disadvantaged by the Scottish and Welsh Assemblies. At the same time, Muslim terrorism may be displaced by re-emerging Irish terrorism; alternatively, Muslim terrorism could escalate in parallel with a Middle East war. Elsewhere, existing conflicts are likely to intensify and other conflicts may be triggered: for example, heated argument over a core EEC principle with human rights implications could prompt an unexpected European war. It is customary for a *war of self-righteousness* to be fought in Flanders during every second turn of the long cycle.

Weathering the storm

Freud suggested that individuals should be offered a useful outlet for their aggression: so should nations. Major construction projects come to mind: much bashing of stone and hauling of loads. Sadly, while pyramid building might have shed aggression in ancient Egypt, and Cathedral building in medieval England, laborious projects are unlikely to appeal to haughty, post-imperial Britons, let alone Europeans preoccupied with global warming.

During the 1970s it was noticeable that both Britons and Americans shed aggression in the way that hamsters do: by jogging. The popularity of jogging increased into the 1980s: the first London Marathon took place in 1981; it is still held every year. Sports scientists and anger management experts might usefully research this avenue of aggression shedding: there is a deep pool of aggression awaiting their attention. In the meantime, everything possible should be done to reduce perceived deprivation. Beyond 2015, it will be the height of folly to tell people that they deserve more, that they are entitled to more, or that someone else has their entitlement to something. A few noisy hotheads could easily inflame the vulnerable population; only a strong national consensus would be able to prevent this leading to a social explosion.

Some oddities

The 1980-88 Iran/Iraq war was nearing its end as I wrote up my research. There had been trench warfare and slaughter reminiscent of WW1 on the wrong side of the violence cycle. This puzzled me at first: eventually I realised that, while oil-rich nations experience the same crisis points, their cycle of economic prosperity may not be in phase with that of the Western democracies. A high oil price constrains the Western democracies but empowers the oil-rich nations. The fuse for the Iran/Iraq war had been lit by the Iranian revolutionaries who seized power in 1979 - the *crisis of disillusionment* - and set up a Shi'ite Islamic state.

The same crisis point prompted the short, sharp 1982 Falklands War. The Argentine President had hoped that, by going to war, he could unify his people in a period of economic turmoil. During similar economic turmoil, in 1876, General Custer's cavalrymen trotted off to their doom beside the Little Bighorn River.

Proof of the pudding

The world keeps turning: situations change. This epilogue will gradually be overtaken by events, at which time you will be able to evaluate my predictions and, hopefully, validate my hypotheses.

12th March, 2007 Terence Parker

The Author

Terence Parker was born in India in 1939, the son of an infantry bandmaster. After short stays in the post-war devastation of London and in Warwick, his family settled in Swansea where he attended Bishop Gore Grammar School.

In 1957, after achieving top marks in the Armed Services Entrance Examination, he entered the Royal Military Academy Sandhurst. Commissioned into REME, he gained an Honours Degree in Electrical Engineering before serving in a variety of appointments in the United Kingdom, Europe and North America.

In 1983, shortly after remote but focal involvement in the Falklands Campaign as the Equipment Manager of Army Guided Weapons, he left the Army to become an administrator at Imperial College in London. Whilst there, he decided to investigate the fundamental cause of war. He completed his purely private research in 1986: a time when few people were interested in war.

In 1989, he rejoined the Ministry of Defence as a civilian, just in time to help prepare Britain's tanks for the first Gulf War. Now retired, he has time to review his research and remember many battlefields visits: Waterloo, Ypres, Gallipoli, Shiloh, Gettysburg, the Indian Mutiny flashpoints and the banks of the Little Bighorn River, to name but a few.